Mother and Daughter Journal

Mother and Daughter Journal

SHARED MEMORIES AND KEEPSAKES

Bluestreak
BOOKS

Bluestreak

an imprint of Weldon Owen International

1045 Sansome Street, San Francisco, CA 94111

www.weldonowen.com

Written and designed by Girl Friday Productions

www.girlfridayproductions.com

Library of Congress Cataloging in Publication data is available.

ISBN: 978-1-68188-463-9

First Printed in 2019

10 9 8 7 6 5 4 3 2 1

2019 2020 2021 2022

Printed and bound in China

Illustration Credits:

©Shutterstock/Viktoriya Yakubouskaya: cover, endsheets, pocket; ©Shutterstock/ Maria_Galybina: cover, 2, 3, 16–17, 30–31, 32, 33, 42, 43, 62, 63, 70–71, 72–73, 74–75, 84–85, 88–89, 90–91, 94–95, pocket; ©Shutterstock/Jung Suk Hyun: 4, 5, 28–29, 60–61, 64–65; ©Shutterstock/Anna Paff: 6, 7, 14, 15, 18–19, 68, 69, 58–59, 78–79; ©Shutterstock/Tania Anisimova: 8–9; ©Shutterstock/Cat_arch_angel: 10–11, 26, 27, 76, 77; ©Shutterstock/love pattern: 12–13, 56–57; ©Shutterstock/lumpra: 14, 15, 68, 69; ©Shutterstock/mejorana: 20–21; ©Shutterstock/Lera Efremova: 22–23, 44–45, 52–53, 66, 67; ©Shutterstock/Irtsya: 24–25, 38–39; ©Shutterstock/Anastasia Lembrik: 34, 35; ©Shutterstock/Anasteisha: 36–37; ©Shutterstock/moobeer: 40–41; ©Shutterstock/Jane_Mori: 46, 47; ©Shutterstock/ Naticka: 48–49, 54, 55, 82–83; ©Shutterstock/mistletoe: 50–51, 80–81; ©Shutterstock/ Anastasia Dzhanaeva: 67; ©Shutterstock/formalnova: 86–87, 96; ©Shutterstock/ Manon_Labe: 92–93

This book is dedicated to

_____

_____

_____

Contents

How to use this book

How you use this book is up to you. Some pages include prompts that may require interviewing one another to discover the answers, while other pages can be filled in separately and then shared later. However you decide to fill the pages, the goal is to share and communicate with each other, and to be able to record these memories in a special place. Some pages include photo frames. In these places, add your own photos or ephemera using photo corners or other photo-safe scrapbooking supplies. If you don't have a photo, use the space to write a vivid description of a person or event. You can even try hand drawing an image instead! There's also an envelope at the back of the book—tuck in keepsakes and memorabilia to preserve them for generations to come.

INTRODUCTION

A Note to Moms and Daughters

You already know that your bond is special. That's why you're each other's favorite TV-watching, ice-cream-eating, clothes-sharing, late-night-talking, movie-going partner in crime. And that's also why there's no one you fight with harder or louder. For all the ups and downs, moms and daughters are the ultimate pairing—and this book is all about you and your relationship. Use these pages to celebrate the shared moments—accomplishments, funny stories, memorable trips—and to talk to each other when things aren't perfect. Capture the memories so they can last forever, honoring one of the most special bonds in your life. Whomever *you* consider to be your mom or daughter, Honor that bond here.

PART ONE

All About Us

ALL ABOUT US

Life began with waking up
and loving my mother's face.
—George Eliot

MOM'S NAME:

DAUGHTER'S NAME: Corinne Stringer

DAY WE MET: My Birthday May 21, 2009, they day I was born.

The moment my mom saw me she:

What my mom remembers most from that moment is:

The moment my daughter saw me she: _____

_____

_____

_____

What my daughter remembers most from that moment is: _____

_____

_____

_____

_____

Here is a photo of us when we first met: _____

My mom was born in: _____

_____

Which is near: _____

_____

Her address growing up was: _____

_____

Her birthday is: _____

_____

Her parents named her (full name): _____

_____

They chose her name because: _____

_____

_____

_____

_____

_____

_____

_____

_____

_____

My daughter was born in: _____

_____

Which is near: _____

_____

Our address when she was born was: _____

_____

Her birthday is: _____

_____

We named her (full name): _____

_____

We chose her name because: _____

_____

_____

_____

_____

_____

_____

_____

_____

Here are some words that describe my mom: _____

_____

_____

_____

_____

My mom's best qualities are: _____

_____

_____

_____

_____

_____

_____

_____

My mom makes me happy when she: _____

_____

_____

_____

_____

_____

_____

_____

Here are some words to describe my daughter: _____

_____

_____

_____

My daughter's best qualities are: _____

_____

_____

_____

_____

_____

_____

My daughter makes me happy when she: _____

_____

_____

_____

_____

_____

_____

What my mom looks like: _____

_____

_____

_____

_____

_____

_____

_____

Her doppelgänger could be: _____

_____

_____

_____

I love it when she wears: _____

_____

_____

_____

_____

_____

_____

_____

What my daughter looks like: _____

_____

_____

_____

_____

_____

_____

Her doppelgänger could be: _____

_____

_____

_____

I love it when she wears: _____

_____

_____

_____

_____

_____

_____

_____

OUR FAVORITE THINGS

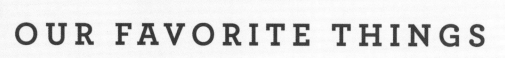

Here are a few of my mom's favorite things: _____

_____

_____

_____

_____

When she really loves something, she does this: _____

_____

_____

I'm happy seeing my mom when she loves something because: _____

_____

_____

_____

Here are a few of my daughter's favorite things: _____

_____

_____

_____

_____

When she really loves something, she does this: _____

_____

_____

_____

I'm happy seeing my daughter when she loves something because: _____

_____

_____

_____

_____

_____

_____

_____

_____

My mom's favorite season is: _____

What she likes about the season is: _____

_____

_____

Something this season always makes her think about is: _____

_____

_____

My mom's favorite color is: _____

She loves it because: _____

_____

_____

My mom's favorite foods are: _____

_____

She likes to eat them at: _____

_____

_____

When she eats them she thinks of: _____

_____

_____

My mom's favorite scent is: _____

_____

_____

_____

My daughter's favorite season is: _____

What she likes about the season is: _____

_____

_____

Something this season always makes her think about is: _____

_____

_____

My daughter's favorite color is: _____

She loves it because: _____

_____

_____

My daughter's favorite foods are: _____

_____

She likes to eat them at: _____

_____

_____

When she eats them she thinks of: _____

_____

_____

My daughter's favorite scent is: _____

_____

_____

_____

PART TWO

Things We Do Together

THINGS WE DO TOGETHER

What the daughter does, the mother did.
—Jewish proverb

HERE ARE A FEW THINGS WE *LIKE* TO DO TOGETHER: _____

_____

_____

_____

_____

_____

HERE ARE A FEW THINGS WE *LOVE* TO DO TOGETHER: _____

_____

_____

_____

_____

OUR GO-TO MOVIE TO WATCH TOGETHER IS: _____

_____

We love to watch this movie because: _____

_____

_____

Our favorite scene is: _____

_____

_____

Some other movies we like to watch together: _____

_____

_____

_____

OUR GO-TO TV SHOW TO WATCH TOGETHER IS: _____

_____

We always watch it: _____

_____

_____

We love it because: _____

_____

_____

Some other shows we like to watch together: _____

_____

_____

WE BOTH ENJOY READING THESE KINDS OF BOOKS, THESE GENRES:

_____

_____

_____

_____

_____

WE LIKE TO READ DURING: _____

_____

_____

_____

_____

The first book my mom read to me was: _____

_____

_____

_____

The first book we read together was: _____

_____

_____

_____

Some of my mom's favorite authors are:

These are the books my mom wants to read:

Some of my daughter's favorite authors are:

These are the books my daughter wants to read:

PLACES WE GO TOGETHER

A special place to visit with my mom is: _____

_____

_____

We go there when: _____

_____

_____

When we are there, we: _____

_____

_____

The reason it is so special: _____

_____

_____

_____

_____

_____

A special place to visit with my daughter is: _____

_____

_____

We go there when: _____

_____

_____

When we are there, we: _____

_____

_____

The reason it is so special: _____

_____

_____

_____

_____

_____

_____

_____

_____

_____

THE RESTAURANT WHERE WE ARE REGULARS IS: _____

_____

When we go there, we always eat: _____

_____

_____

We go there when we: _____

_____

_____

A memorable moment from eating there was: _____

_____

_____

_____

_____

_____

Other restaurants we like are: _____

_____

_____

_____

_____

_____

OUR MOST MEMORABLE VACATION WAS: _____

_____

_____

_____

WE WENT THERE ON: _____

WHILE WE WERE THERE, WE: _____

_____

_____

_____

My daughter has fond memories of this part of the trip: _____

_____

_____

_____

My mom has fond memories of this part of the trip: _____

_____

_____

_____

OUR FAVORITE SHARED MEMORY FROM THE TRIP WAS: _____

_____

_____

_____

_____

HOBBIES WE ENJOY

An enjoyable hobby I do with my mom is: _____

_____

_____

_____

_____

I love doing this with her when: _____

_____

_____

_____

It feels special because: _____

_____

_____

_____

_____

An enjoyable hobby I do with my daughter is:

_____

_____

_____

I love doing this with her when: _____

_____

_____

_____

It feels special because: _____

_____

_____

_____

_____

_____

_____

_____

WHAT WE LISTEN TO

WE SOMETIMES HAVE DIFFERENT MUSICAL TASTES BUT WE BOTH LIKE

LISTENING TO: _____

_____

_____

_____

WE LIKE IT BECAUSE: _____

_____

_____

_____

SOME SONGS THAT WE BOTH LIKE TO LISTEN TO: _____

_____

_____

_____

_____

_____

My mom introduced me to these musical artists: _____

_____

_____

_____

_____

_____

My favorite songs by these artists are: _____

_____

_____

_____

_____

_____

My daughter introduced me to these musical artists: _____

_____

_____

_____

_____

My favorite songs by these artists are: _____

_____

_____

_____

PART THREE

What We
Talk About

WHAT WE TALK ABOUT

The mother's heart is the child's schoolroom.
—Henry Ward Beecher

HERE ARE SOME OF THE TOPICS WE LIKE TO TALK ABOUT MOST: _____

_____

_____

_____

_____

HERE ARE SOME OF THE TOPICS WE DON'T LOVE TALKING ABOUT: _____

_____

_____

_____

_____

I like to talk to my mom when I'm feeling: _____

_____

_____

We have our best talks when we are: _____

_____

_____

The time of day I like to talk to my mom is: _____

_____

_____

_____

_____

_____

I like to talk with my daughter when I'm feeling: _____

_____

_____

We have our best talks when we are: _____

_____

_____

The time of day I like to talk to my daughter is: _____

_____

_____

_____

The funniest story my mom ever told me was: _____

_____

_____

_____

_____

_____

_____

_____

_____

_____

Something that always makes my mom laugh is: _____

_____

_____

_____

_____

_____

_____

_____

The funniest story my daughter ever told me was: _____

_____

_____

_____

_____

_____

_____

_____

_____

_____

Something that always makes my daughter laugh is: _____

_____

_____

_____

_____

_____

_____

_____

_____

The hardest thing I ever talked about with my mom was: _____

_____

_____

_____

_____

_____

_____

Talking about it made me feel: _____

_____

_____

_____

_____

After talking with my mom, I felt: _____

_____

_____

_____

_____

The hardest thing I ever talked about with my daughter was: _____

_____

_____

_____

_____

_____

_____

_____

Talking about it made me feel: _____

_____

_____

_____

_____

_____

_____

_____

After talking with my daughter, I felt: _____

_____

_____

_____

_____

_____

My mom and I always agree about: _____

_____

_____

_____

_____

_____

We never agree about: _____

_____

_____

_____

_____

_____

When we don't agree, we: _____

_____

_____

_____

_____

_____

My daughter and I always agree about: _____

_____

_____

_____

_____

_____

_____

We never agree about: _____

_____

_____

_____

_____

_____

_____

_____

When we don't agree, we: _____

_____

_____

_____

_____

_____

_____

_____

Something my mom is really passionate about is: _____

_____

_____

_____

_____

_____

_____

I know something is really important to her when she: _____

_____

_____

_____

_____

_____

_____

Something we are both passionate about is: _____

_____

_____

_____

_____

_____

_____

Something my daughter is really passionate about is:

_____

_____

_____

_____

_____

I know something is really important to her when she:

_____

_____

_____

_____

_____

_____

Something we are both passionate about is:

_____

_____

_____

_____

_____

When my mom is upset, she: _____

_____

_____

_____

_____

_____

_____

_____

_____

When my mom is upset, I try to help by: _____

_____

_____

_____

_____

_____

_____

_____

_____

When my daughter is upset, she:

When my daughter is upset, I try to help by:

WE COMMUNICATE BEST WHEN WE:

WE LAUGH THE MOST WHEN WE ARE:

WHEN WE FEEL QUIET WE LIKE TO: _____

_____

_____

_____

_____

_____

_____

_____

WHEN WE CELEBRATE SOMETHING WE: _____

_____

_____

_____

_____

_____

_____

_____

_____

This is a card my mom wrote me when: _____

_____

This card is special to me because: _____

_____

_____

This is a card my daughter wrote me when: _____

_____

This card is special to me because: _____

_____

_____

_____

_____

_____

_____

_____

_____

_____

_____

_____

_____

_____

_____

_____

WHAT WE TEACH
EACH OTHER

My mom's best life lesson for me is: _____

_____

_____

_____

_____

I always trust my mom's opinion about: _____

_____

_____

My mom always reminds me that it's important to: _____

_____

_____

The best advice my mom ever gave me was: _____

_____

_____

_____

My daughter's best life lesson for me is: _____

_____

_____

_____

_____

I always trust my daughter's opinion about: _____

_____

_____

_____

My daughter always reminds me that it's important to: _____

_____

_____

_____

The best advice my daughter ever gave me was: _____

_____

_____

_____

_____

PART FOUR

My Mom and Me, Past and Future

MY MOM AND ME, PAST AND FUTURE

A mother's happiness is like a beacon, lighting up the future
but reflected also on the past in the guise of fond memories.

—Honoré de Balzac

Some of my hopes for my mom are: _____

_____

_____

_____

_____

_____

_____

_____

_____

_____

Some of my hopes for my daughter are: _____

_____

_____

_____

_____

_____

_____

_____

_____

_____

_____

_____

_____

_____

_____

_____

_____

_____

_____

_____

_____

FAVORITE MEMORIES

My most cherished memory with my mom is: _____

_____

_____

_____

_____

This memory is so special because: _____

_____

_____

_____

_____

When I think about this memory I feel: _____

_____

_____

My most cherished memory with my daughter is: _____

_____

_____

_____

_____

This memory is so special because: _____

_____

_____

_____

_____

When I think about this memory I feel: _____

_____

_____

_____

_____

_____

_____

_____

This is a photo from a memorable trip with my mom:

When we took this photo, we were: _____

_____

_____

I love this photo because: _____

_____

_____

_____

_____

_____

This is a photo from a memorable trip with my daughter:

When we took this photo, we were: _____

_____

_____

I love this photo because: _____

_____

_____

_____

_____

The best trip my mom and I ever took together was: _____

_____

_____

_____

_____

I loved this trip because: _____

_____

_____

_____

_____

A vivid memory from this trip was: _____

_____

_____

_____

_____

_____

_____

_____

The best trip my daughter and I ever took together was:

_____

_____

_____

_____

I loved this trip because:

_____

_____

_____

_____

_____

A vivid memory from this trip was:

_____

_____

_____

_____

_____

_____

_____

The funniest thing my mom and I ever did together was: _____

_____

_____

_____

_____

_____

_____

_____

_____

It was so funny because: _____

_____

_____

_____

_____

_____

_____

_____

_____

The funniest thing my daughter and I ever did together was: _____

_____

_____

_____

_____

_____

_____

_____

_____

It was so funny because: _____

_____

_____

_____

_____

_____

_____

_____

_____

The scariest thing my mom and I ever did together was: _____

_____

_____

_____

_____

_____

_____

_____

It was so scary because: _____

_____

_____

_____

_____

_____

_____

_____

The scariest thing my daughter and I ever did together was: _____

_____

_____

_____

_____

_____

_____

_____

_____

It was so scary because: _____

_____

_____

_____

_____

_____

_____

_____

_____

_____

MAKING NEW MEMORIES

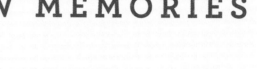

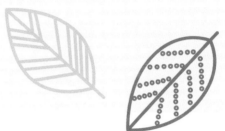

THESE ARE SOME OF THE THINGS WE'D LOVE TO DO TOGETHER SOMEDAY:

THIS IS AT THE VERY TOP OF OUR WISH LIST: _____

I'd love to visit this place with my mom: _____

_____

_____

Here's why I think she'd love it: _____

_____

_____

_____

_____

_____

These are some of the things we'd love to do there: _____

_____

_____

_____

_____

_____

_____

_____

_____

_____

_____

_____

I'd love to visit this place with my daughter: _____

_____

Here's why I think she'd love it: _____

_____

_____

_____

_____

These are some of the things we'd love to do there: _____

_____

_____

_____

_____

_____

_____

_____

One wish I have for my mom's future is:

One wish I have for my daughter's future is: _____

_____

_____

_____

_____

_____

_____

_____

_____

_____

_____

_____

_____

_____

_____

_____

_____

_____

_____

_____

STANDOUT MOMENTS

Something special that my mom has accomplished is: _____

_____

_____

_____

_____

_____

_____

_____

_____

_____

When I think about my mom doing this, I feel: _____

_____

_____

_____

Something special that my daughter has accomplished is: _____

_____

_____

_____

_____

_____

_____

_____

_____

_____

When I think about my daughter doing this, I feel: _____

_____

_____

_____

_____

_____

_____

_____

_____

_____

Something my mom did that makes me proud is: _____

_____

_____

_____

_____

_____

_____

_____

_____

I feel proud because: _____

_____

_____

_____

_____

_____

_____

_____

_____

Something my daughter did that makes me proud is:

_____

_____

_____

_____

_____

_____

_____

_____

I feel proud because:

_____

_____

_____

_____

_____

_____

_____

_____

The hardest thing my mom ever did was: _____

_____

_____

_____

_____

_____

_____

_____

_____

When I think about her doing this, I feel: _____

_____

_____

_____

_____

_____

_____

_____

The hardest thing my daughter ever did was: _____

_____

_____

_____

_____

_____

_____

_____

When I think about her doing this, I feel: _____

_____

_____

_____

_____

_____

_____

_____

_____

PART FIVE

Letters to Each Other

LETTERS TO EACH OTHER

Letters are among the most significant memorial
a person can leave behind them.

—Johann Wolfgang von Goethe

SOMETIMES IT'S EASIER TO WRITE WHAT YOU'RE
FEELING THAN TO SAY IT. IN THESE PAGES WE GIVE
YOU THE CHANCE TO WRITE TO EACH OTHER—EVEN
WHEN THE WORDS DON'T COME EASILY.

SOMETIMES WE ARE SO FOCUSED ON THE PRESENT WE DON'T TALK
ABOUT OUR HOPES AND DREAMS FOR THE FUTURE. USE THIS SPACE TO
WRITE WHAT YOU HOPE THE FUTURE HOLDS FOR EACH OTHER. WHAT
WOULD MAKE YOU MOST PROUD? WHY? WHAT WORDS OF ADVICE OR
WISDOM DO YOU WANT TO PASS ON?

DEAR _____

_____

_____

_____

LOVE _____

DEAR

LOVE

DEAR

LOVE

DEAR

LOVE

IT CAN BE DIFFICULT TO SAY WHAT WE FEEL MOST DEEPLY. USE THIS SPACE TO TELL EACH OTHER WHAT YOU TREASURE MOST ABOUT EACH OTHER. WHAT ARE THE QUALITIES YOU VALUE IN ONE ANOTHER OVER ANY OTHER? WHY IS THIS RELATIONSHIP IMPORTANT IN YOUR LIFE?

DEAR

LOVE

DEAR

LOVE

DEAR

LOVE

DEAR

LOVE

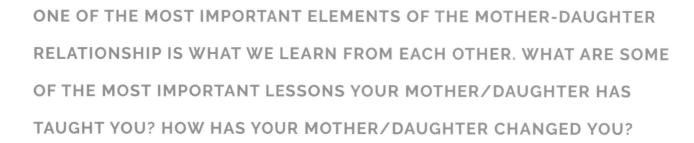

ONE OF THE MOST IMPORTANT ELEMENTS OF THE MOTHER-DAUGHTER RELATIONSHIP IS WHAT WE LEARN FROM EACH OTHER. WHAT ARE SOME OF THE MOST IMPORTANT LESSONS YOUR MOTHER/DAUGHTER HAS TAUGHT YOU? HOW HAS YOUR MOTHER/DAUGHTER CHANGED YOU?

DEAR

LOVE

DEAR

LOVE

DEAR

LOVE

DEAR

LOVE

A HOPE I HAVE FOR YOU IS . . .

DEAR

LOVE

DEAR

LOVE

DEAR

LOVE

DEAR

LOVE

AS MUCH AS WE LOVE EACH OTHER, SOME THINGS ARE HARD TO TALK ABOUT. HERE ARE SOME SPACES TO WRITE THE THINGS THAT ARE HARD TO SAY OUT LOUD.

DEAR _____

_____

_____

_____

_____

_____

_____

_____

LOVE _____

DEAR _____

_____

_____

_____

_____

_____

_____

LOVE _____

DEAR

LOVE

DEAR

LOVE

FAVORITE PHOTO OF US TOGETHER

WE TOOK THIS PHOTO IN: _____

THIS PHOTO IS SO SPECIAL BECAUSE: _____

_____

_____

_____

_____